SCIENCE FUN WITH TOY CARS AND TRUCKS

Rose Wyler
Pictures by Pat Stewart

JULIAN MESSNER ⓂⓎ NEW YORK
A Division of Simon & Schuster, Inc.

JULIAN MESSNER and colophon are trademarks of Simon & Schuster, Inc.
10 9 8 7 6 5 4 3 Lib. ed.
10 9 8 7 6 5 4   Pbk. ed.

Manufactured in the United States of America
Design by Lisa Hollander

Library of Congress Cataloging in Publication Data
Wyler, Rose
Science fun with toy cars and trucks.

Summary: Demonstrates scientific principles such as propulsion and inertia
with easy activities using toys.
1. Science–Experiments–Juvenile literature.
(1. Science–Experiments. 2. Experiments) I. Title.
Q164. W86 1988   507'.8   87-20326
ISBN 0-671-63784-3 Lib. ed.
ISBN 0-671-65854-9 Pbk. ed.

FOREWORD

Science provides a way of looking at the world around you and trying to understand how things work. Toy cars can help explain how real cars and other things move. The experiments in this book will show you how forces like gravity and friction work. The experiments are safe and easy to set up at home or at school. They are so much fun, you will want to try them all. Your parents will too!

Lewis Love
Great Neck Public Schools
Long Island, New York

ACKNOWLEDGMENTS

The author and publisher wish to thank the people who read the manuscript of this book and made suggestions: Lewis Love, Great Neck, New York, Public Schools; Dr. Richard Leigh, Professor of Physics, Pratt Institute, Brooklyn, New York; Gerald Ames; and the many young "helpers" who tried the experiments.

OTHER BOOKS BY ROSE WYLER

The Giant Golden Book of Astronomy
Prove It!
Secrets in Stones [all written with Gerald Ames]
Science Fun with Drums, Bells, and Whistles
Science Fun with a Homemade Chemistry Set
Science Fun with Mud and Dirt
Science Fun with Peanuts and Popcorn
Science Fun with Toy Boats and Planes

CONTENTS

FINISH

6

Wheels at Work

Driving a car is easy, if it's a toy car. Just push it, or start the motor if it has one. The wheels turn and the car moves.

What kind of a car do you have? A small model? A big car that runs on batteries? A homemade truck? Have you put your car through any test drives? Test-driving is exciting. It is also a way of doing science experiments that show how a real car works. After all, a toy car is like a real car in many ways.

The road is open. Let's get started!

Rolling Along

Push a box across the floor. You can move it, but it drags. The whole bottom of the box rubs against the floor. This rubbing is *friction.* It makes the box drag and slow down.

If you put the box on a roller skate, it's easy to move. The wheels make all the difference. They roll along.

The skate and box work together like a toy car.

CUT ALONG
HEAVY LINES

To make a toy car, start with a 2-quart milk carton. Ask a grown-up to cut off the top and one side of the carton so it becomes an open box. Put two slits in it on opposite sides. Run a string through the slits. Now tie the box on a roller skate. And there's your car. Give the car a push and it rolls along.

To rig the car like a truck, make a cab from a piece of the carton. Use fasteners to hold the cab in place. The picture shows how to do this.

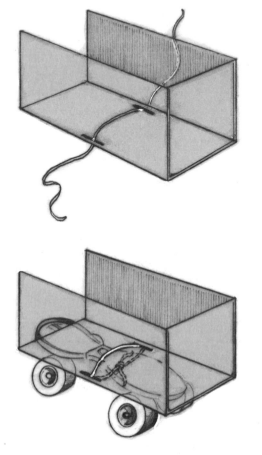

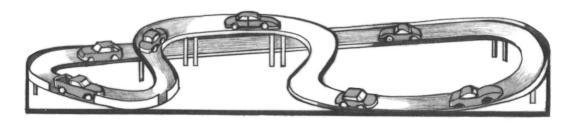

Why Wheels Are Round

Watch the wheels of your car as they turn and turn. Just how do they move the car?

Wheels can roll because they are round. One part of the rim after another comes down, then lifts up. Only a small part touches the ground. There is very little rubbing—very little friction. So the car moves easily.

But that's only part of the story.

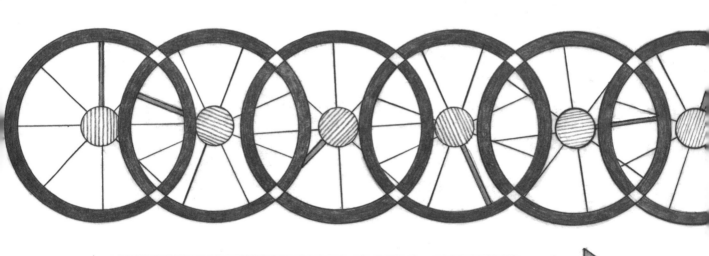

Moving Forward

Car wheels move by pushing against the ground. To go forward, the wheels push backward. If the road could move, the car would push it back. Here's proof this would really happen.

To make a road, lay a strip of card-board on a smooth floor. Use a toy car that has a wind-up motor or an electric motor. Set the car on the strip, start the motor, and watch the "road" slip back.

Turn the car around and run it over the strip again. Now which way does the road go?

When the car pushes the road, the road pushes in the opposite direction. And that make the car move.

Action and Reaction

Pushes always come in pairs. A push is a force—an action. It starts a push in the opposite direction—a reaction. When a car or anything else moves, both pushes are at work.

If you push a toy car into a wall, what happens? The car bounces back. The wall pushes it back. The wall hits the car with as much force as the car used in hitting it.

Set a toy car on a smooth floor and draw a short chalk line in front of the first two wheels. Give the car a push to send it against the wall. See how far back it goes after it hits the wall. Then mark the spot where it stops.

Now repeat the experiment with the car at the same starting point, but give it a harder push. This time the car goes back farther, doesn't it? The wall reacts with more force because the car hits it with more force.

Even if your car is a toy, its wheels work like a real car's wheels. Action by the wheels and reaction by the road makes them go.

Starting and Stopping

A car needs force—a push or a pull—to start it. If the car has a motor, the motor starts it. If it's a toy car with no motor, you push or pull it by hand.

Force is needed to stop a car, too. A car would keep on moving forever unless some force stopped it. Even your toy car would keep on moving. That may be hard to believe. But try these experiments and see for yourself.

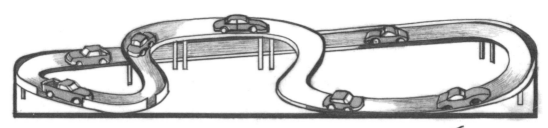

Lazy Cars

Set a toy car on a piece of cardboard. Then quickly pull away the cardboard. The car stays in place.

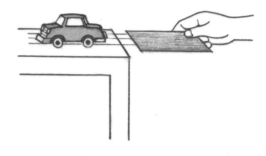

Take two small trucks that are alike. Load one to make it heavy. Push each truck with the finger of one hand. Which truck feels harder to move? The heavy truck?

The truck seems too lazy to move. Scientists call this laziness *inertia*. When you start a car, you have to work against inertia. The heavier a car is, the more inertia it has, and the harder it is to start.

When a Doll Is a Passenger

Keeping a car moving is easy once the car has started. Even if the motor stops or you stop pushing, the car will coast for a while. Now it seems too lazy to stop. Inertia is at work again.

Anything that's inside the car acts lazy, too. It tends to keep on moving along with the car. To prove this, give your car a test drive with a doll sitting inside.

Use a small doll or make one with modeling clay. Set the doll down in the car. Then drive the car. Stop it suddenly and the doll falls forward suddenly.

Head the car the other way and stop it again. Now which way does the doll fall?

Try this, too. Make the car back up. Then force it to stop suddenly. See what happens to the doll.

You will find that the doll always falls in the direction in which the car is moving. Both the car and doll seem to want to keep on moving. Both have inertia.

Seat Belts

Everything and everybody has inertia. Watch yourself when you ride in a car. If the car stops suddenly, you fall forward. A seat belt will hold you back. A seat belt keeps you safely in place, and that's why you should use one.

Using string, or ties from plastic bags, rig a seat belt for a doll. Then give this dummy a ride in a toy car to see how the seat belt works. Stop the car suddenly. Does the seat belt keep the dummy from falling forward?

18

Red Light—Stop!

The light turns red and traffic has to stop. Stopping is like starting—it takes force. The heavier a car is, the harder it is to stop. Here's an experiment that shows this.

Take two toy cars—a light car and a truck with a heavy load. Set them side by side. With the help of a friend, get them moving at the same speed. Then put a hand in front of each one. The heavy truck is harder to stop, isn't it? The heavy truck has more inertia than the light one. That's why more force is needed to stop it.

How Brakes Work

Inertia can keep a car moving for a while—but not for long. Parts inside the car rub against each other, and the wheels rub against the road. All this friction finally stops the car.

To stop a car quickly, friction has to be developed quickly. A brake does this job. On a toy car, you can use a stick for a brake. While the car is moving, press the stick against one of the wheels. The stick rubs against it and makes enough friction to stop the car.

In a real car, the brake works in the same way, but it is under the body. The brake presses against the inside of the wheels or against a part that turns the wheels. This causes so much friction that the car stops.

On the Road

When cars were invented about a hundred years ago, roads were bad. They were made for horses and carriages. Early cars looked like carriages, too. They had high bodies and big wheels. Engines were weak and cars often broke down. When they got stuck, people yelled, "Get a horse!"

How different cars are now, with smooth, low bodies that hug the road. Big engines give them power and speed. Roads are paved and built so that traffic can move along quickly. Yet driving isn't easy.

You will see why as you test-drive toy cars over ice and sand, uphill, downhill, and around curves.

21

Slippery When Wet

A film of water on a road makes it smooth and slippery. When the wheels touch water instead of the road, there is less friction and the car may skid.

Driving on Ice

An icy road is more slippery than a wet one. It's even hard to drive a toy car on ice. Try it outdoors on a cold day, using a car with a motor. See if it skids on ice.

If there is no ice, put a big tray of water in the freezer of a refrigerator and freeze it. Then start the car's motor and test-drive it over the ice. Can you figure out how to keep the car from skidding?

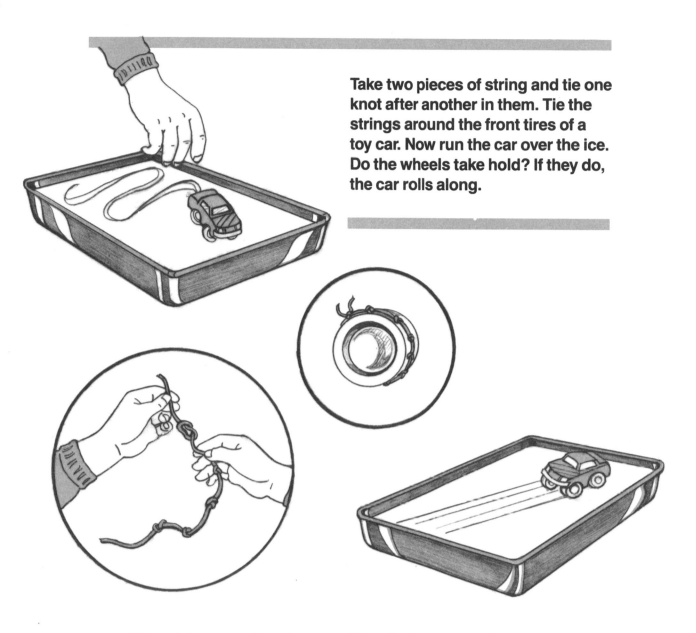

Take two pieces of string and tie one knot after another in them. Tie the strings around the front tires of a toy car. Now run the car over the ice. Do the wheels take hold? If they do, the car rolls along.

The strings on the tires act like chains on real car tires. When roads are icy, many drivers use chains. Or they use snow tires. Snow tires have treads that give them a good grip on smooth roads.

In winter, sand is sometimes spread over an icy road. How much does this help? Sprinkle some sand on ice. Then see if your toy car travels over it without skidding.

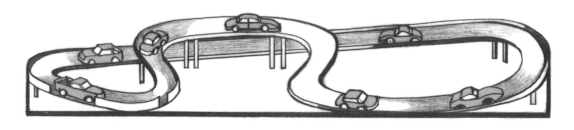

Beach Buggies and Jeeps

A little sand can be helpful, but driving over a sandy beach or a desert is another matter. A car's wheels can sink in the sand and get stuck. To prevent this, drivers use beach buggies or jeeps with big, wide tires. The wheels press down on the sand, but the big tires spread out the pressure. This keeps the wheels from sinking.

Stuck in the Mud

Another problem for drivers is slippery mud. If wheels can't get a grip on the mud, they just spin, and the car is stuck.

That can happen to a toy car, too. Run a model with a motor over a stretch of mud. If the car gets stuck, you can pull it out, of course. But is there some other way to get the car out of the mud?

Try a method that drivers of real cars use. Push flat stones under the wheels of your toy car. Then start the motor. If the wheels take hold on the stones, the car gets over the muddy strip.

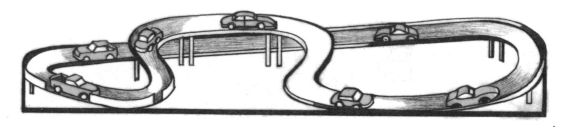

Going around Curves

On many models of toy cars, each pair of wheels is fixed on a rod—an axle. The axle turns and the two wheels turn with it. One wheel can't turn without the other. The car can't go around a curve because the outside wheels must go farther and faster.

Hold your car upside down and see how the wheels are set on the axle. Then tie a string to the car. Pull it in a circle and see if any of the wheels drag.

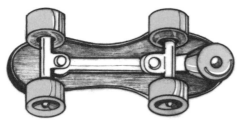

The best toy car for experiments on curving roads is a truck built on a roller skate. Pull the truck in a circle and watch the wheels. You can see that each wheel turns separately. That's the way the wheels of a real car work.

The truck will move around a curve easily if you steer it. But why do you have to steer it? The answer may surprise you. The truck will go in a straight line unless you force it to turn. Anything that's moving goes straight, if it can.

Seat a doll in the middle of a truck and give her a ride around a curve. Watch her carefully. She slides to one side, doesn't she? As she slides, she tends to keep going in a straight line.

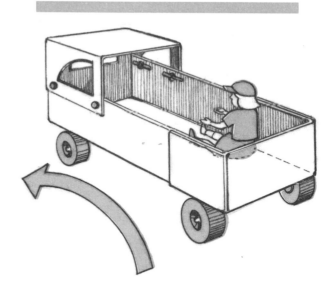

It seems that the doll doesn't want to go around the curve. Inertia makes her act that way. The truck has inertia, too. And that's why force is needed to make it turn.

Inertia makes it hard to stop the truck. Once it starts moving, it keeps on moving for a while. If the truck has been going around and around in a circle, will it keep on doing that? Which way will it go?

To mark the truck's path, tape a piece of chalk on the front of the skate. Place it as in the picture. Now tie a long cord to the middle of the truck. Set the truck on a smooth floor. Hold the cord tight and whirl the truck around in a circle. When it's moving fast, let go of the cord. Zing! the truck shoots off, straight as an arrow. Behind it is a record of its path—a circle with a straight line coming from it.

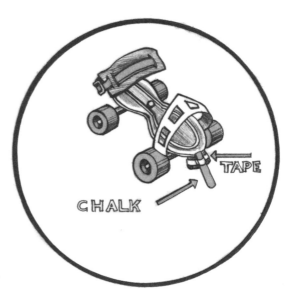

TAPE

CHALK

The minute you drop the cord, you stop forcing the truck to turn around curves. The truck is free to go straight ahead—and it does.

A real car rounds a curve the way a toy truck does. It tends to keep going straight. But the driver steers it to make the car wheels turn.

Nowadays, highways are built to help cars stay on winding roads. Guard rails are placed along the turns. Roads are also tilted a little so that the outside edge of a curve is higher than the inside. Signs with snaky lines warn drivers, too. They mean: Danger! Curves ahead.

29

Uphill, Downhill

Did you ever run a toy car over a hilly road? Try it, using a long board for the road. To make the road slope like a hill, set one end of the board on a few books.

Watch the car coast downhill. It seems to be moving on its own. But the car is being pulled downward by the earth's gravity. Gravity pulls everything downward. In fact, it makes things fall unless they are held in place.

To drive uphill, you have to work against gravity and use force. If the car has a motor, see if the motor will pull it up the slope. Or pull it by hand.

How hard do you have to pull to make the car climb? Do you have to use more force if the slope is steeper?

You can find out by pulling the car with a rubber band. The rubber band acts as a meter. The more force that pulls on it, the more the rubber band stretches.

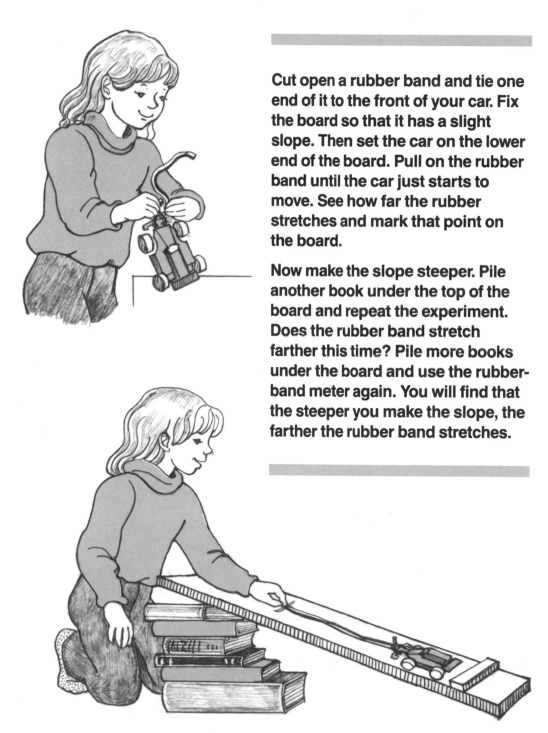

Cut open a rubber band and tie one end of it to the front of your car. Fix the board so that it has a slight slope. Then set the car on the lower end of the board. Pull on the rubber band until the car just starts to move. See how far the rubber stretches and mark that point on the board.

Now make the slope steeper. Pile another book under the top of the board and repeat the experiment. Does the rubber band stretch farther this time? Pile more books under the board and use the rubber-band meter again. You will find that the steeper you make the slope, the farther the rubber band stretches.

Try different cars on the sloping road, too. Use a strong rubber band for the meter if you test a truck with a heavy load. You will find that it takes a lot of force to drive a heavy car uphill. Pulling against gravity is hard work.

Watch a real giant trailer truck climb a steep hill. How much force it takes! The engine chugs and tugs and finally the truck gets over the top. It's a wonderful machine.

Your homemade truck is wonderful, too, in its own way. And so is every toy car that can go up and down hills.

REPAIR JOBS

Does Toytown have a service station? Why not start one? Of course, toy cars don't need the service and repairs that real cars need. But you can pretend they do.

For the shop, use a big cardboard carton. You can keep the tools for repairs in the carton. You will want a tow truck, too. But there's no need to buy one. Just load your homemade truck with some cord and clips and you'll be able to handle toy-car tow jobs.

When everything is ready, put up your sign: OPEN FOR BUSINESS.

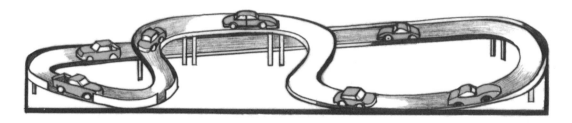

Good-bye to Squeaks

Squeaks are annoying. They can also mean something is wrong. If you find out what causes them, you can stop them. Try this.

Take two stones and rub them together. As the grains of the stones move against each other, they grate and squeak. Feel the stones. They're warm—a sign of friction.

Now cover part of each stone with cooking oil to fill in the spaces between the grains. Rub the smooth, greasy parts against each other. You will find they move quietly and easily, for there's less friction.

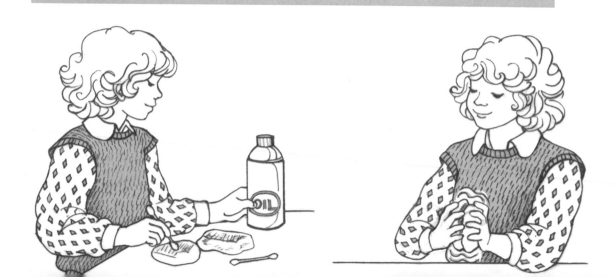

Well, here comes Bill, driving his rattling old car. "Can you fix it?" he asks.

In a toy car, wheels sometimes squeak as they move around the axle. Is that the trouble with Bill's car? To find out, you turn the car upside down. You spin the front wheels, and sure enough, they squeak. The rear wheels squeak, too. So you put a drop of oil between each wheel and axle. You spin the wheels again, and now they turn quietly.

Bill test-drives his car. The squeaks are gone, and the car runs easily. "Runs like a new car," says Bill. "You did a fine job."

Car Lift

Sometimes a real car needs a lube job. Ask a grown-up to take you into a service station to see how this job is handled.

The car is placed over a big metal shaft. A motor makes the shaft rise from the floor. Up it comes, lifting the car.

Now a man can stand underneath. He quickly gets to work, shooting in grease where it is needed. When he has finished, the car is lowered and it is ready for the road.

It's easy to rig up a lift for toy cars. The lift won't be like one used for real cars. But it will be fine for make-believe repairs.

You will need a plastic cup and a cardboard tube about 4½ inches long. A toilet-paper tube will work best. If you have a longer tube, ask a grown-up to cut it down. Also ask the grown-up to cut the bottom off the cup. Then fit the tube in it. After you stand the cup upside down, set a car on top of the tube. Move the tube up and the car goes up, too. It is ready for greasing.

Call for the Tow Truck

The phone is ringing. There's trouble down the road. Sue's car has skidded into a wall. The tow truck is ready. Toytown Service to the rescue!

You tow Sue's car to your repair shop. You can fix some of the damaged parts, but others have to be replaced.

Where do you get parts for Sue's car? Maybe from an old car that was broken up for parts. Sometimes real cars are repaired with used parts.

So keep your old cars and ask your friends to keep theirs, too. Then you can swap cars and parts. You can even build a good car from old parts. That's more fun than buying a new car.

LOADING AND UNLOADING

Moving day! Heavy furniture must be loaded on a van.

Supplies arrive for the supermarket! Stacks of cartons must be unloaded from trailer trucks.

Movers and truck drivers are strong. But they are not strong enough to do all that lifting with their own muscles. They use machines.

You, too, can use lifting machines in your trucking business —things like ramps and rollers. Easy does it!

Ramp Experiments

When you load your truck, you lift a weight against gravity. Lifting it straight up is the hard way. Instead, use a ramp. With a ramp, you raise the weight the same height from the ground, but you raise it a little at a time.

Use a slat of wood or stiff cardboard for the ramp. Rest one end on the ground and the other end on the truck bed. Then tape it in place.

For the weight, tie a string around a smooth stone. Loop the end of the string around your pinky and lift the stone straight up. You will find it's quite heavy. Now set the stone on the ramp and pull it up into the truck. This is easier, isn't it?

Whichever way you raise the stone, its weight and the pull of gravity are the same. So about the same amount of force is needed. But when you use the ramp, you exert this force a little at a time, for the ramp is the longer way up. You never pull as hard as when you lift the stone straight up.

The ramp always supports part of the stone's weight as you pull. There's less strain on your muscles, and the work is easier.

Watch a truck take on a heavy load and you are likely to see workers using a ramp. The ramp is a great invention.

Ramps are used to lower things as well as to lift them. A heavy carton will slide down a ramp if there is not too much friction. To cut down the friction, rollers are used on some ramps. As the rollers turn, they move the weight along.

To see how rollers work, place four pens close together on a table. Set a small box on them and give the box a little push. It moves easily because the rollers turn like wheels. Take away the rollers and you have to give the box a harder push to make it move.

You can make a ramp with rollers for your toy truck, but you will need a grown-up friend to help you a little.

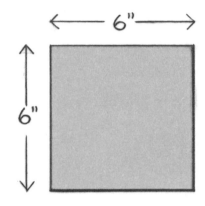

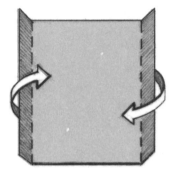

FOLD ON DOTTED LINES

Start with a square of cardboard about 6 inches on each side. Bend over the edges on two opposite sides, as shown in the picture. These edges will be the sides of your ramp. Have your friend cut four holes about an inch apart in each side. Put a pen through each pair of holes, and now you have a ramp with rollers.

Set the ramp against the bed of your truck and tape it in place. Try to move a little box up the ramp and down it. Try some stones, too. How well do the rollers work? Do they help move the weight along?

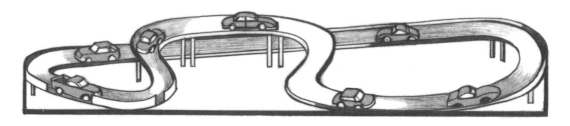

Lifting with a Pulley

A pulley is sometimes used to lift heavy things. Here's how you can make one.

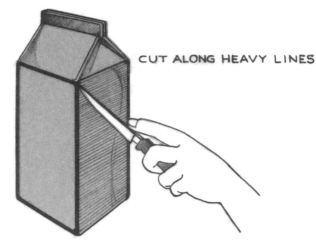

CUT ALONG HEAVY LINES

First make a frame from a milk carton. Ask a grown-up to cut off the top and two opposite sides. Punch a hole in each side that's left. Punch them near the top. Work a pen through the holes and the frame is finished. To keep it from toppling, set a weight on the bottom.

For the pulley, you need a spool, a paper clip, and a tie from a plastic bag. Straighten the clip and run it through the spool. Bring the ends together and use the tie to fix them to the pen. If the spool turns easily, the pulley is ready for a lifting job.

Take a string about 2 feet long. Tie a small box to one end. Lead the other end of the string over the spool. Pull down the loose end of the string and up comes the box.

Pulling down is easier than pulling up when lifting a weight. That's why the pulley is a good lifting machine.

To use the pulley in your truck, stand the frame in the back of the truck and weigh down the bottom. Now you're ready for a heavy loading job. Your truck can be a wrecker with a pulley to hoist toy cars. Beep beep! Here it comes.

The Big Little-Car Rally

By now you are an expert toy-car driver, and so are many of your friends. Why not have a rally and show each other your skills?

Find a place where you can lay out a road with curves, hills, holes, and some mud. Then you and your friends can take turns driving uphill and down, over good stretches and bad. At the same time, everyone can sing this round. It's to the tune of "Row, Row, Row Your Boat":

**Drive, drive, drive your car
Up and down the run.
Merrily, merrily, merrily, merrily,
Let's have Science Fun.**

START

BIG LITTLE-CAR RALLY

How about giving the best drivers blue ribbons to put on their cars? You could give awards, too, for the oldest car, the best homemade truck, and the best repair job. Every driver should get a badge saying: Toy Car Expert.

   End your rally in style with a parade of toy cars. As the cars move along, there will be noisy horns and cheering, showing that the Big Little-Car Rally is a great success.

After the rally, drive your car into the garage—that is, a box. Keep it ready for more driving and more work. You will think of many ways to have Science Fun as you try new experiments with your toy car.